Materials

Paper

Chris Oxlade

Heinemann
LIBRARY

www.heinemann.co.uk/library
Visit our website to find out more information about **Heinemann Library** books.

To Order:
Phone 44 (0) 1865 888066
Send a fax to 44 (0) 1865 314091
Visit the Heinemann Library Bookshop at www.heinemann.co.uk/library to browse our catalogue and order online.

First published in Great Britain by Heinemann Library, Halley Court, Jordan Hill, Oxford OX2 8EJ a division of Reed Educational and Professional Publishing Ltd.
Heinemann is a registered trademark of Reed Educational & Professional Publishing Ltd.

OXFORD   MELBOURNE   AUCKLAND   JOHANNESBURG   BLANTYRE
GABORONE   IBADAN   PORTSMOUTH (NH)   USA   CHICAGO

Designed by Storeybooks
Originated by Ambassador Litho Ltd.
Printed in Hong Kong / China

ISBN 0 431 12725 5 (hardback)   ISBN 0 431 12732 8 (paperback)
05 04 03 02 01   06 05 04 03 02
10 9 8 7 6 5 4 3 2   10 9 8 7 6 5 4 3 2 1

British Library Cataloguing in Publication Data
    Oxlade, Chris
    Paper. – (Materials)
    1. Paper
    I. Title
    620.1'97

Acknowledgements
Corbis pp 14, /Philip Gould p.4, /Jacqui Hurst p.23, /Paul Seheult/Eye Ubiquitous p.26, /Ron Watts p.18; DIY Photo Library p.24; Elizabeth Whiting Associates p.25; Jacqui Hurst p.17; Photodisc pp.19, 20, 21, 27; Powerstock Zefa pp.11, 16, 28; Science Photo Library /Colin Cuthbert p.15, /Microfield Scientific Ltd. p12, /Tommaso Guicciardini p.13; Tudor Photography pp. 5, 6, 7, 8, 9, 10, 22.

Cover photograph: Heinemann Library.

Every effort has been made to contact copyright holders of any material reproduced in this book. Any omissions will be rectified in subsequent printings if notice is given to the Publisher.

Contents

What is paper? 4

Strong and weak 6

Paper and card 8

Wet and dry 10

Making paper 12

Drying and rolling 14

Writing and painting 16

Printing on paper 18

Paper packaging 20

Paper objects 22

Paper in homes 24

Recycling paper 26

Fact file 28

Would you believe it? 29

Glossary 30

More books to read 32

Index 32

You can find words shown in bold, **like this**, in the Glossary.

What is paper?

Paper is made in workshops and
factories. It is not a **natural** material.
This paper has just been made. It is
stored on rolls, ready to be made into
newspapers.

Paper has many uses. Most paper is made
into newspapers, books and magazines. It
is also used for bags and wrapping. All the
things in this picture are made from paper.

Strong and weak

Paper is easy to scrunch up into a ball. It is also easy to tear into pieces. A sheet of paper is quite strong, though, if you try to stretch it or pull it apart.

A sheet of paper can be made much stiffer by folding it. This girl is using a paper fan to keep cool. The fan is stiff because of the folds in the paper.

Paper and card

There are many different kinds of paper. The paper in this book has a smooth, shiny **surface**. Other types of paper have a rough surface. Some are coloured with dyes.

Card is thick, stiff paper, normally with a smooth surface. It comes in different thicknesses. **Cardboard** is very thick and stiff. One kind has a wavy sheet of card in the centre. This makes it even stiffer.

Wet and dry

Paper towels and handkerchiefs are made of paper that soaks up **liquid** very well. The liquid flows into tiny spaces inside the paper.

Paper containers for liquids are made
from paper that does not soak up water
at all. The paper is covered with a thin
layer of **wax** or plastic.
This stops the water
going through
the paper.

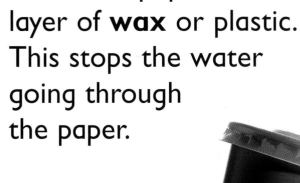

Making paper

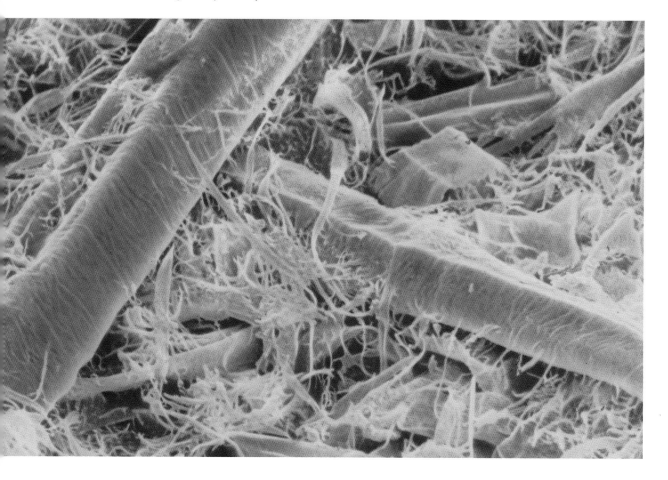

Paper is made from tiny **fibres** that come from plants. You can see the fibres when you tear paper. Most fibres used for making paper come from wood. The wood comes from trees.

Paper is made at a **factory** called a **paper mill**. Wood is mixed with water and **chemicals**. Then it is mashed up by machines to make wood **pulp**. It looks like a thick paste.

Drying and rolling

The runny wood **pulp** is poured onto a wire mesh, which works like a large, flat sieve. The mesh catches the woody fibres but lets the water drain away. This makes a layer of wet paper.

The wet paper is taken off the mesh. Then the rest of the water is squeezed out by heavy rollers and the paper is dried. The finished paper is put on big rolls, or it is cut into sheets.

Writing and painting

Paper for writing has a smooth **surface**.
The surface is covered in **chemicals**.
They stop the ink from a pen soaking
into the paper and becoming blotchy.

This painting is being done on thick paper that soaks up watery paints. The paper is called water-colour paper. It will dry out when the painting is finished.

Printing on paper

Most paper is used for **printing**. It is made into newspapers, books and magazines. This paper is going through a newspaper **press**.

Bank notes are printed on paper that has strong **fibres** in it. This makes the paper difficult to tear. The notes last for more than a year before they wear out.

Paper packaging

Many packaging materials are made from paper. Gift wrapping paper often has patterns printed on it. Paper bags are made by folding and gluing paper.

Cardboard is used to make strong boxes. The boxes protect things inside. A flat piece of cardboard is folded to make a box shape. The edges of the cardboard are joined with glue or metal **staples**.

Paper objects

Many objects are made by cutting, folding and gluing paper. These boxes and aeroplanes are made from thin card and paper.

This plate is made from a material called papier mâché. You make papier mâché by mashing up wet paper and glue. It goes very hard when it dries.

Paper in homes

The walls of this home are being decorated with wallpaper with a raised pattern on it. The wallpaper is thick and heavy. It is being pasted to the walls.

In some Japanese homes, screens made of wood and paper are used instead of walls between rooms. Sheets of paper are glued onto wooden frames to make screens and sliding doors.

Recycling paper

Millions of trees are cut down every day to make paper. **Paper mills** use lots of electricity. Trees and electricity can be saved by using paper again. This is called recycling.

Paper sent for recycling is mashed up to make wood **pulp**. Ink from **printing** is removed from the pulp with **chemicals**. Most recycled paper is used to make newspapers and **cardboard**.

Fact file

▶ Most paper is made in **factories**. It is not a **natural** material.

▶ Paper is easy to scrunch into a ball and tear.

▶ Paper is hard to stretch and pull apart.

▶ Paper can be made stiffer by folding it.

▶ Paper can be smooth or rough. It can be white or coloured.

▶ **Card** is thicker and stiffer than paper.

▶ Some kinds of paper are waterproof. Some kinds soak up water.

▶ Paper does not let electricity or heat flow through it.

▶ Paper burns when it is heated.

▶ Paper is not attracted by **magnets**.

Would you believe it?

Paper for newspapers comes on huge rolls as tall as a grown-up person and as heavy as a family car. If a roll was unrolled, it would be about 15 kilometres long. It would take a grown-up three hours to walk that far!

Glossary

card thick, stiff paper with a smooth surface

cardboard very stiff, thick material made from layers of card and paper

chemicals special materials that are used in factories and homes to do jobs like cleaning and protecting

factory place where things are made using machines

fibre thin thread or tiny piece of a material. Paper fibres come from the trees or plants the paper is made from.

liquid substance that flows, such as water and oil

magnet object that attracts iron or steel

natural comes from plants, animals or rocks in the earth

paper mill factory where paper is made

press machine that prints inks onto paper

printing making patterns, words or pictures on paper by pressing ink onto the paper

pulp mixture of wood and water that has been mashed together

staple piece of metal wire that sticks through sheets of paper, card or cardboard, joining them

surface top or outside of an object

wax material that feels smooth and oily and does not let water through. Candles are made of wax.

More books to read

Materials: Wood
Chris Oxlade
Heinemann Library, 2001

What are...? Forests
A. Owen and M. Ashwell
Heinemann Library, 1998

Step-by-Step: Papermaking
David Watson
Heinemann Library, 2000

I Can Help Recycle Rubbish
Franklin Watts

Science Explorers: Paper
A & C Black, 1999

Index

card 9, 22, 28
cardboard 9, 21, 27
chemicals 13, 16, 27
factory 4, 13, 28
fibres 12, 19
folding 7, 22, 28
newspaper 4, 5, 29
painting 17
paper bags 5

paper mill 13, 26
papier mâché 23
printing 18, 27
pulp 13, 14, 27
screens 25
surface 8, 16
wallpaper 24
wrapping paper 5, 20
writing 6

Titles in the *Materials* series include:

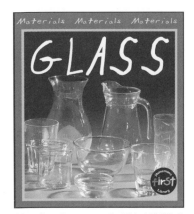

Hardback   0 431 12723 9

Hardback   0 431 12722 0

Hardback   0 431 12725 5

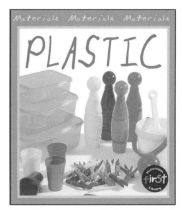

Hardback   0 431 12721 2

Hardback   0 431 12720 4

Hardback   0 431 12724 7

Find out about the other titles in this series on our website www.heinemann.co.uk/library

This
Treasure Cove Story
belongs to

CAPTAIN MARVEL

A CENTUM BOOK 978-1-912841-47-9
Published in Great Britain by Centum Books Ltd.
This edition published 2020.

1 3 5 7 9 10 8 6 4 2

Centum Books Ltd, 20 Devon Square, Newton Abbot,
Devon, TQ12 2HR, UK.

www.centumbooksltd.co.uk | books@centumbooksltd.co.uk
CENTUM BOOKS Limited Reg. No. 07641486.

A CIP catalogue record for this book is available
from the British Library.

Printed in China.

Centum

A *Treasure Cove* Story

MARVEL
CAPTAIN MARVEL

By John Sazaklis
Illustrated by Penelope R. Gaylord

CAPTAIN MARVEL is an interstellar Super Hero. She protects all planets in the galaxy – especially her home planet, Earth!

Captain Marvel is really Carol Danvers.
She was once an air force captain.
She could **FLY** higher…

Carol Danvers even went on secret missions in outer space. She once caught an alien spy stealing a mysterious device.

Carol stopped the thief, but the device **EXPLODED**! She was zapped by a strange energy that gave her special abilities.

With her new powers, Carol Danvers became **CAPTAIN MARVEL**.

Captain Marvel is **INCREDIBLY FAST**…

...and **STRONG**!

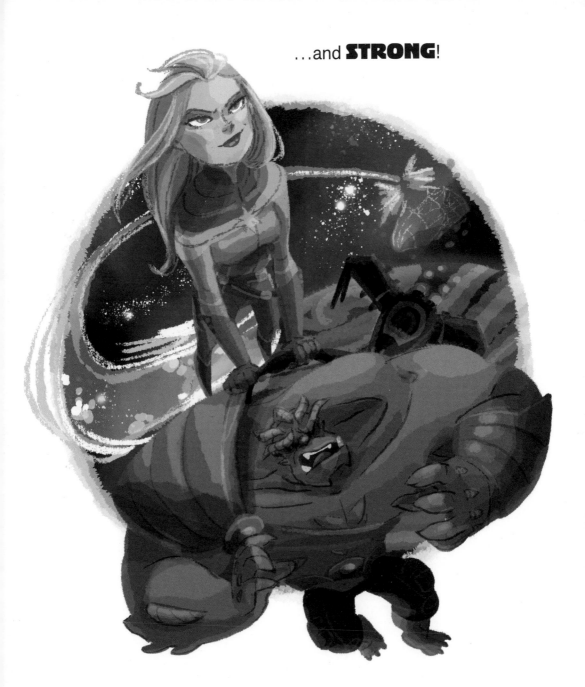

She easily catches intergalactic bad guys...

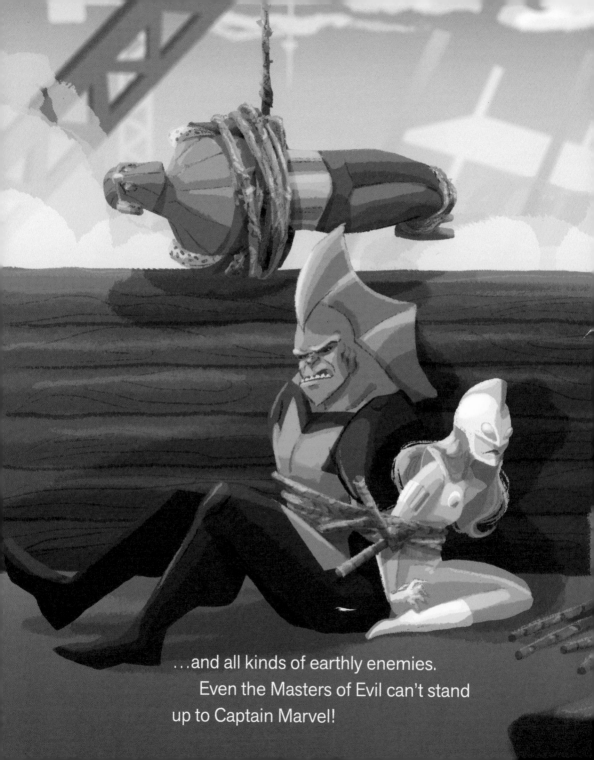

...and all kinds of earthly enemies.
Even the Masters of Evil can't stand
up to Captain Marvel!

Uh-oh! A kitten is in trouble. Not every rescue
Captain Marvel makes involves aliens… *or does it?*
This ball of fur is really an alien **FLERKEN**.

The Flerken's foe is quickly defeated – and Captain Marvel adopts the cuddly critter.

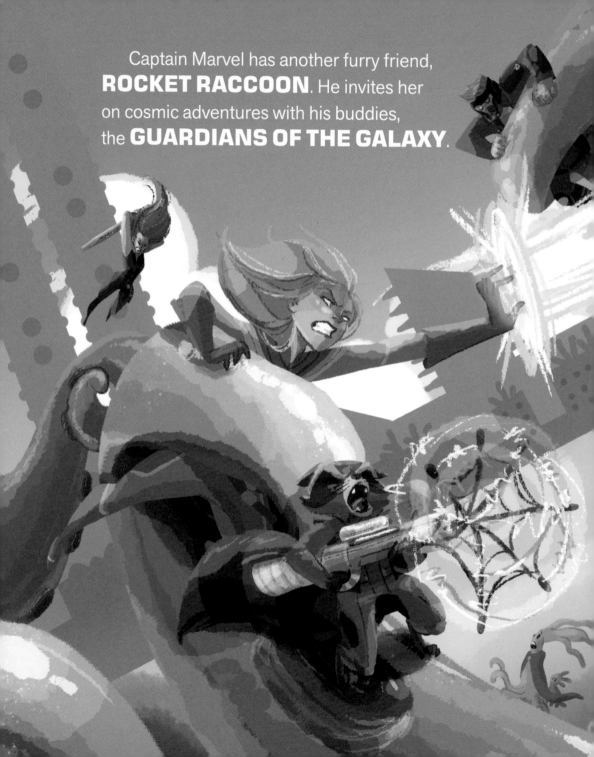

Captain Marvel has another furry friend, **ROCKET RACCOON**. He invites her on cosmic adventures with his buddies, the **GUARDIANS OF THE GALAXY**.

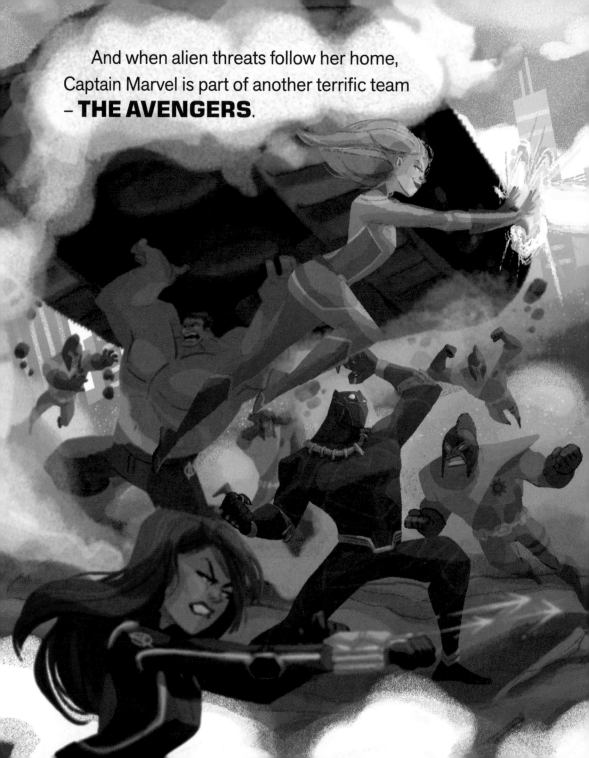

And when alien threats follow her home,
Captain Marvel is part of another terrific team
– THE AVENGERS.

RONAN THE ACCUSER invades Earth, but he finds that the **KREE** army is no match for Captain Marvel and the mighty Avengers.

By working as a team, the heroes win again!

Captain Marvel is
an inspiration to people
everywhere…

...especially to a girl named **KAMALA KHAN**. This stretchy, shape-shifting super teen named herself **MS MARVEL** in honour of her idol.

On Earth or in space, Captain Marvel
is a hero who is out of this world.

GO, CAPTAIN MARVEL!

Treasure Cove Stories

Please contact Centum Books
to receive the full list of titles in
the *Treasure Cove Stories* series.
books@centumbooksltd.co.uk

Classic favourites

1 Three Little Pigs
2 Snow White and
the Seven Dwarfs
3 The Fox and the Hound
- Hide-and-Seek
4 Dumbo
5 Cinderella
6 Cinderella's Friends
7 Alice in Wonderland
8 Mad Hatter's Tea Party
from Alice in Wonderland
9 Mickey Mouse and
his Spaceship
10 Peter Pan
11 Pinocchio
12 Mickey and the Beanstalk
13 Sleeping Beauty
and the Good Fairies
14 The Lucky Puppy
15 Chicken Little
16 The Incredibles
17 Coco
18 Winnie the Pooh and Tigger
19 The Sword in the Stone
20 Mary Poppins
21 The Jungle Book
22 The Aristocats
23 Lady and the Tramp
24 Bambi
25 Bambi - Friends of the Forest

Recently published

50 Frozen
51 Cinderella is my Babysitter
52 Beauty and the Beast
- I am the Beast
53 Blaze and the Monster Machines
- Mighty Monster Machines
54 Blaze and the Monster Machines
- Dino Parade!
55 Teenage Mutant Ninja Turtles
- Follow the Ninja!
56 I am a Princess
57 The Big Book of Paw Patrol
58 Paw Patrol
- Adventures with Grandpa!
59 Paw Patrol - Pirate Pups!
60 Trolls
61 Trolls Holiday
62 The Secret Life of Pets
63 Zootropolis
64 Ariel is my Babysitter
65 Tiana is my Babysitter
66 Belle is my Babysitter
67 Paw Patrol
- Itty-Bitty Kitty Rescue
68 Moana
69 Nella the Princess Knight
 - My Heart is Bright!
70 Guardians of the Galaxy
71 Captain America
- High-Stakes Heist!
72 Ant-Man
73 The Mighty Avengers
74 The Mighty Avengers
- Lights Out!
75 The Incredible Hulk
76 Shimmer & Shine
- Wish Upon a Sleepover
77 Shimmer & Shine - Backyard Ballet
78 Paw Patrol - All-Star Pups!
79 Teenage Mutant Ninja Turtles
- Really Spaced Out!
80 I am Ariel
81 Madagascar
82 Jasmine is my Babysitter
83 How to Train your Dragon
84 Shrek
85 Puss in Boots
86 Kung Fu Panda
87 Beauty and the Beast - I am Belle
88 The Lion Guard
- The Imaginary Okapi
89 Thor - Thunder Strike!
90 Guardians of the Galaxy
- Rocket to the Rescue!
91 Nella the Princess Knight
- Nella and the Dragon
92 Shimmer & Shine
- Treasure Twins!
93 Olaf's Frozen Adventure
94 Black Panther
95 Trolls
- Branch's Bunker Birthday
96 Trolls - Poppy's Party
97 The Ugly Duckling
98 Cars - Look Out for Mater!
99 101 Dalmatians
100 The Sorcerer's Apprentice
101 Tangled
102 Avengers
- The Threat of Thanos
103 Puppy Dog Pals
- Don't Rain on my Pug-Rade
104 Jurassic Park
105 The Mighty Thor
106 Doctor Strange

Latest publications

107 Captain Marvel
108 The Invincible Iron Man
109 Black Panther
- Warriors of Wakanda
110 The Big Freeze
111 Ratatouille
112 Aladdin
113 Aladdin - I am the Genie
114 Seven Dwarfs Find a House
115 Toy Story
116 Toy Story 4
117 Paw Patrol - Jurassic Bark!
118 Paw Patrol
- Mighty Pup Power!
119 Shimmer & Shine
- Pet Talent Show!
120 SpongeBob SquarePants
- Krabby Patty Caper
121 The Lion King - I am Simba
122 Winnie the Pooh
- The Honey Tree
123 Frozen II
124 Baby Shark and the
Colours of the Ocean
125 Baby Shark and
the Police Sharks!
126 Trolls World Tour

Book list may be subject to change.